Diamond & Sky

Written and illustrated by Marilyn Hoobler

Mare's Field Publishing
9 Warrenton Drive
Silver Spring, Maryland 20904
©2009 All rights reserved.

No part of this book may be reproduced, stored in a retrieval system,
or transmitted by any means without the written
permission of the author.

First published by Mare's Field Publishing, April 2009
ISBN: 978-0-9822066-0-7
Printed in the United States of America
LaVergne, Tennessee U.S.A. 37086

for Carey,
for his love, patience,
and encouragement
&

for Dr. Fred Lewis, DVM
for his time and devotion
to animals and their humans

A Colt Is Born

Not long after his birth, a colt wandered over to an old gelding in the field. The gelding pinned his ears. No young colt belonged at his shoulder. He was in charge!

The colt didn't bat an eye. His coat was golden and smooth. On his forehead was a perfect white diamond. His mane and tail were white too.

He didn't move away from the grumpy horse.

Kick! Kick! The gelding's feet flew like hammers.

The colt's lip bled, and he lost a tooth. His shoulder hurt too. But he lowered his head to graze on the spring clover.

The old gelding moved away. Why pick a fight with this little nobody?

The colt was given the name Diamond. He grew strong and won ribbons at horse shows. Then at an auction, a man looked him over.

"This horse is handsome and does well in shows," he said. "And he loves to run. I think I'll race him."

For many years Diamond ran in long races against bigger horses. Sometimes he won. He rode in parades too.

One day a woman came to visit the barn where Diamond lived. She loved to ride.

"Let's go," the man said. "You can borrow Diamond." They rode across fields, through woods, over bridges, and through streams.

At the end of the day the man said, "He likes you. If I decide to sell that horse, you can buy him."

"He's nice and small," she said. "I could share him with my children."

After that, the woman sometimes looked at other horses to buy, but she didn't choose one. Finally the man called. Did she want to buy Diamond?

Yes!

Diamond got used to a new barn and new fields and trails.

When the woman brought her sons to the barn, she put Justin, who was five, up on Diamond. He sat straight and tall. It looked as though he had grown right out of the horse's back.

"This is how you turn," she said.

Justin listened to his mother. Diamond listened to him.

"Good job. You'll make a fine rider someday."

Judah looked up at his brother. On Diamond's back, he looked taller than their mother. "I want to be up there! I want to ride!"

"Diamond is a small horse," the mother said. "But he's too big for you."

A few days later, while Justin was in school, the mother took Judah for a long drive. When they were in the mountains, she turned onto a small road that led up to a farm. A pony trotted to the fence to greet them.

Her small ears pricked forward. Her fluffy winter coat made her look like a snowball with large brown spots.

"She has one brown eye and one blue eye!" Judah shouted.

"Maybe that's why they named her Sky," the mother said.

"How did you know that was her name?"

The mother smiled.

The owner let them groom the pony with a brush. When they finished, he took Sky to a large, round pen.

"This is how I trained her," he said, flicking his hand toward the pony. Sky walked, then trotted, then cantered in each direction. When the owner held up his hand, Sky came to a fast stop.

The pony knew how to listen.

"Now let's see what she'll do for you," the owner said to the mother as he stepped out.

Sky watched the mother. She stood in the center of the round pen and held up her hand. Flicking her wrist, she said, "Walk on."

Sky hesitated.

The mother took a step toward her. Sky decided to walk on. Each thing the owner had asked Sky to do, the mother asked of her as well. Each time Sky obeyed.

"She listens well enough to you," the owner said. "You keep her calm.

But, the little boy . . . I don't know."

The mother shook hands with Sky's owner. "We'll be back with the trailer to get her."

When Diamond and Sky met, Diamond did not behave like the grumpy gelding he had met as a colt. He sniffed Sky from head to tail and let out a happy snort. She responded with a squeal, and they grazed together on sweet grass.

Two animals now needed washing, brushing, combing, and riding. The work seemed like it would never stop. But Justin and Judah learned to care for the horses and to ride, and the horses learned to listen.

Judah and Sky

After school each day, Justin's dad took him to play football.

Judah couldn't go. He wasn't old enough for football.

Judah groused.

"It's good you cannot go," his mother said. "You'll get a head start learning to ride the pony."

But he wanted to play football.

"Never mind. You'll be a good rider."

Judah was not so sure. Until now, he had only ridden Sky in the round pen with his mother leading her, but he'd seen the pony run in the pasture. She was fast. Could he ride that fast?

"Don't you worry. I have a surprise," the mother said.

Judah saddled Sky. Rummaging sounds came from inside the tack room of the barn where his mother dug into a wooden trunk. Judah stood on tiptoe.

Peering into the window, he tried to see into the room. His mother pulled out two leather straps with rubber circles on them and what looked like a very long lead rope. "Take her to the arena," she called out.

In the arena, the mother began attaching the straps to the girth on Sky's saddle and the long line to her bridle.

"What are these for?"

She smiled. She tightened the girth and tied the reins to the front of the saddle. "Climb on."

Judah climbed on as his mother held the stirrup on the opposite side.

"You won't be using the reins," she said.

His eyes widened.

"This saddle we've been using is a lunging saddle. The straps I put on the girth are called side reins. I'll attach them to the bit when you ride. And when we lunge, I control the horse using the long line, while you learn to ride. If you don't feel secure, hold onto the grab strap on the front of the saddle."

Judah leaned forward and grabbed the strap.

"Walk on," his mother said, stepping back.

Sky walked forward. The long lead attached to her bridle kept her moving in a wide circle.

"Let's get her warmed up."

"She is warm," Judah said, sitting stiffly.

"I mean her back."

"Her back is warm too," he said.

"Not the muscles," the mother said. "She hasn't been carrying a boy all day. Activate your hips."

"Huh?"

"Move your hips with her as she walks."

Judah moved his hips wildly back and forth in the saddle.

"Too much!" the mother laughed. "Relax. I've trained her to do this."

Judah glanced nervously at his mother. "When?"

"When I come out to ride Diamond. You can't keep riding her in the round pen. She'll get bored. Sit up."

Judah tried closing his eyes and feeling the pony's movement. Slowly he relaxed. Soon, he could ride with his arms out to the side. He could ride with his feet out of the stirrups. He could ride standing in the stirrups. He could lean forward and touch his toes and reach back and pat Sky's tail. He could even spin around and ride backward. All at a walk, of course.

Within the week he had learned to trot. He could now ride in two-point, with his seat out of the saddle, leaning forward with his head and chest up. He could post at the trot. He learned that his seat should rise when Sky's shoulder to the outside of the arena was rising. That was called "posting on the correct diagonal."

He cantered, but he didn't like it. He had watched Sky running like that in the field, and it looked exciting. But it was too fast.

Soon Judah was able to ride on his own without the lunging saddle and the lunge line to his mother. He could control Sky all by himself. Each day his mother set up cones and poles in the arena to make a new pattern of obstacles for them to ride through. Each day they improved.

"Let's go for a hack," his mother said one afternoon.

"What's a hack?"

"That's when you ride in the fields or the woods. I'll keep Sky on a lead rope and walk along with you."

Judah felt ready. They walked through the woods near the barn until they came to a steep hill. As they started to climb it, the mother stopped. "Hmm," she mused. "This hill might—"

Suddenly five deer crashed through the woods. Sky reared. It wasn't a very high rear, but it was enough to make Judah lose his seat. Holding onto the mane, he swung down, landing squarely on his feet.

"A perfect dismount," his mother said. "Let's get her off this hill."

Judah moved closer to his mother and watched Sky.

"It's important you get back on."

Carefully, Judah mounted up and they walked home.

Before long, Judah could ride Sky as he followed his mother, riding Diamond. He saw new things each day: box turtles, toads, chipmunks, and deer. Sky learned not to be startled when things happened. Riding through the

 field one afternoon, they heard what sounded like a toddler crying. "What is it?" Judah asked.

"Let's go look." They picked their way through the brush at the edge of the field. The sound got louder and more urgent. Sky stepped on a branch. At the sound of the crack, the bawling stopped for a moment. Then, through the branches leapt a tiny fawn, its mouth wide open and bleating. It ran straight toward Judah and Sky and stopped two feet away. Looking up, it stood frozen, then bolted away.

"Ha!" the mother laughed. "It thought you were its mother!"

"Will she get lost?"

The fawn disappeared into the tall grass.

"Not likely. Its mother probably saw the whole thing." Sure enough, in

the next pasture stood an anxious doe, flicking her ears nervously. "Let's leave quietly so we won't disturb them."

Once, while riding in the arena, Judah shouted, "Mom, come here!"

"In a minute," she said as she concentrated on teaching Diamond something.

"No, I mean, look."

Diamond minced along the fence with his hindquarters turned slightly in.

"Mom, come now!"

"What?"

"Look."

When at last she trotted toward Judah, the mother saw two vultures sitting on the pasture fence. They ruffled their dull, shaggy feathers. Both slender heads looked sore, with red welts and tiny menacing eyes.

"Ugh."

"Let's ride around and get a better look," Judah said.

"Ok, but be ready for Sky to be startled when she gets close to them."

"I will be."

Inside the pasture, Judah and Sky got very close. Without warning, one vulture opened his wings and began to flap them. Tip to tip, they were as wide as Sky was long, head to tail. As the bird began to fly, Sky bolted. Judah stayed on.

"Turn her back to face the other bird," his mother called.

Judah obeyed and, as the next bird took flight, Sky remained calm.

"She trusts that you are a good leader."

DIAMOND IN DANGER

One afternoon, as Justin was riding Diamond, he noticed something wrong. "He feels bumpy," he said. "Like when the car had a flat tire."

The vet came to see Diamond. "He's hurt his foot, and I'll have to give him a shot to keep him from getting an infection." He thumped his fist twice on Diamond's rump and plunged a needle through the thick hide. Diamond didn't seem to feel it.

"Don't ride him," the vet said.

Each day Diamond got worse. First, the sole of his foot, which should have been stiff and hard like a rock, became soft and moveable like the leather on a football that has gone flat. If you pushed on one side, the other side bulged out. Then both hind feet became soft. Because his feet ached, Diamond lay down most of the time.

Day after day, the vet came to give him medicine and shots. "I'm afraid your horse is very sick. The problem in his feet is called 'founder.'"

He taught the mother and the boys how to soak Diamond's feet and then wrap them up to keep them clean and dry.

Soon Diamond was just a skinny horse, lying under a tree.

"Will he live?" Justin asked the vet.

"Encourage him and don't give up. He can make it."

Still, they were not sure how things would go.

From a pen nearby, Sky munched her hay and watched Justin and Judah and the mother as they took turns caring for Diamond's feet. The boys also took turns riding Sky.

One bright day, they drove up to the barn. Justin went over to ride Sky first thing.

Judah and the mother grabbed the bucket of supplies for Diamond. Down the hill they walked to the loafing shed, which stood right next to the arena.

Usually the boys waved to each other while one was riding Sky in the arena and the other was helping with Diamond. But on this day, Judah didn't look toward the arena at all. Diamond lay stretched out on the ground, not moving.

"Is he dead?"

"He's just resting."

"How do you know?"

"Look." The mother pointed at Diamond's nose, faintly quivering.

A loud noise pierced the air. "Wheeeee!" Justin shrieked as he cantered down the long side of the arena, his arms stretched out as if he were flying.

Diamond's eyes blinked wide open, his head popped up, and he jumped to his feet! Everyone laughed.

From that day, Diamond's hooves began slowly to grow hard again. His feet began to feel better.

But he had been lying down for so many months that he liked it now. It was easy.

"Keep him moving," the vet said.

"How can we do that?" the mother asked. "We're not always here."

"There is your help." The vet pointed to Sky, standing by the fence. Her ears were pricked up.

Sky moved into Diamond's pen. They were each given a pile of hay. At first, Sky ate from her own pile. After a few minutes, she leaned over to look at Diamond's pile. Was his hay better than hers? She had to find out. She would have just one bite.

Diamond chased her away.

Sky moved back to her pile of hay, but soon she leaned over to sniff Diamond's pile. She had to have just one more bite. Every few minutes she tried again.

Diamond was very busy guarding his hay. There was no time to rest, and he began to get stronger.

The leaves fell and covered the ground, and then snow fell. Diamond and Sky stood close to each other to keep warm.

One day in the spring, Diamond stood in the field. The whistle blew to call the horses in to eat.

They began to run, as they did every day, and Diamond watched, as he did every day. They all ran, Sky with them. Diamond lifted his head. He snorted. He stomped. He screamed a shrill bugle call and, spinning around,

he raced to the barn. Passing every horse, he beat them all.

"Hooray!" everyone cheered. "Diamond's running!

Diamond could be ridden again. And that made him strong and fast once more.

Through spring, summer, winter, and fall that year, and another year too, the mother rode Diamond, and Justin and Judah took turns riding Sky.

*Special thanks
to those who helped Diamond
during his illness:*

Hank May

Vicki & Al Coleman

Jacki Edens

Mary Ann Sabin

Jared, Justin, and Judah

&

especially

Sharon Day

www.ingramcontent.com/pod-product-compliance
Lightning Source LLC
LaVergne TN
LVHW081545060526
838200LV00048B/2227